The Hermetic History Of The Akkadians

A. S. Raleigh

Kessinger Publishing's Rare Reprints

Thousands of Scarce and Hard-to-Find Books on These and other Subjects!

- Americana
- Ancient Mysteries
- Animals
- Anthropology
- Architecture
- Arts
- Astrology
- Bibliographies
- Biographies & Memoirs
- Body, Mind & Spirit
- Business & Investing
- Children & Young Adult
- Collectibles
- Comparative Religions
- Crafts & Hobbies
- Earth Sciences
- Education
- Ephemera
- Fiction
- Folklore
- Geography
- Health & Diet
- History
- Hobbies & Leisure
- Humor
- Illustrated Books
- Language & Culture
- Law
- Life Sciences
- Literature
- Medicine & Pharmacy
- Metaphysical
- Music
- Mystery & Crime
- Mythology
- Natural History
- Outdoor & Nature
- Philosophy
- Poetry
- Political Science
- Science
- Psychiatry & Psychology
- Reference
- Religion & Spiritualism
- Rhetoric
- Sacred Books
- Science Fiction
- Science & Technology
- Self-Help
- Social Sciences
- Symbolism
- Theatre & Drama
- Theology
- Travel & Explorations
- War & Military
- Women
- Yoga
- *Plus Much More!*

**We kindly invite you to view our catalog list at:
http://www.kessinger.net**

THIS ARTICLE WAS EXTRACTED FROM THE BOOK:

Shepherd of Man: An Official Commentary on the Sermon of Hermes Trismegistos

BY THIS AUTHOR:

A. S. Raleigh

ISBN 1564594939

READ MORE ABOUT THE BOOK AT OUR WEB SITE:

http://www.kessinger.net

OR ORDER THE COMPLETE
BOOK FROM YOUR FAVORITE STORE

ISBN 1564594939

Because this article has been extracted from a parent book, it may have non-pertinent text at the beginning or end of it.

CHAPTER III

THE AKKADIANS.

The first colony to be established by the Mayas was that of Akkad. In the very beginning of Maya Civilization, only a short time after the landing of the Mayas in Yucatan and long before the sinking of Poseidonis, a party of Missionaries set out from Mayach. The mission was one of Education, Religion and Commerce. The Mayas being an aggressive and conquering race, they sought expansion in every direction. They came to the coast of Western Asia. A party of explorers sailed along the coast of the Indian Ocean to the Persian Gulf and thence up to its head. There seven of them landed under the command of Oannes (he who dwells on the water). However, we must not make the mistake of taking this in too literal a sense. The fact that they were commanded by Oannes simply means they were a seafaring people, and as the natives of the country were dwellers on the land they would give the name Oannes to any people who came from over the seas. Also the number 7 is rather suspicious. This is one of the most sacred numbers to the Mayas and to all other Mystical Peoples, and hence we are justified in looking for a mystical meaning in the number. Seven being the number of completion, we are to understand that this was a thoroughly equipped colony that settled here. They had with them an organized Priesthood, a Civil Government and an Educational system, as well as a thorough Commercial establishment. This party of Colonists went ashore and were the first Maya Colonists to land on Asiatic Soil. The landing was made at the mouth of the Tigris.

They ascended that river to its confluence with the Euphrates. Entering that river, they followed its course of about sixty-five miles and founded their first settlement in the marshy lands, to which, on account of the nature of the soil, they gave the name Akal, a Maya word meaning swamp or marsh. In the course of time this word became altered to Akkad, and therefore the name Akkadians was given to the dwellers in the marshy lands at the mouth of the Euphrates. These details, or the most important of them, are also to be found in the work of Berosus.

They surrounded their settlement with a palisade of reeds for protection against the lions that abounded in those marshes, and also for defense against the aborigines of the alluvial plains of Mesopotamia. Their settlement thus enclosed they called "the enclosed place," or Kalti, from the Maya "kal" (enclosed) and "ti" (place). In course of time the aborigines, changing the "t" into a "d," called them Kaldi, by which nickname their tribe continued to be known in after times, when as Caldeans they became numerous and powerful, having acquired great influence through their learning.

In a short time after the establishment of this settlement there were several thousand other Mayas who came here and settled, and in time the city of Akkad or Akal became a great emporium for ships, which traded with all the outlying countries, and thus in time it became the greatest maritime center in all the Eastern Hemishpere. In this way was built up a great Commercial Empire, the seat of which was Akkad. In time this city dominated all of what was later known as Lower Chaldea. This city was in fact the capital of the entire country and became the favorite burial place for all those anywhere near. It is now known as Mugheir. In their tombs they used the pointed triangular arches which were used in Mayach, and which characterize Mayan Civilization wherever it may be found. Not only was this true of the construction of the tombs, but the position of the bodies was identically the same as that in which they were placed in Yucatan. Loftus, "Chaldae and Susiana," page 134, gives this description, which is quite accurate, of the position of the bodies: "The body was laid upon the matting. It was commonly turned upon its left side, the right arm falling toward the left and the fingers resting upon the edge of a copper bowl, usually placed in the palm of the left hand." To understand the significance of this practice we must bear in mind that the Mayas placed the body on the left side, with the right hand resting on the left shoulder, if he were a man of some distinction. The bowl was the symbol of the vase, which was supposed to contain the man's good deeds. It was in fact, what Theosophists would call the receptacle of the Man's Karma that was to go over to his use in the after death state and also in future births. This vase for the reception of the man's good deeds was the measure of his justification, and hence it was the Vase of Justification. Among the Mayas it was resting on the stomach or rather the abdomen, in many cases. Among the Akkadians the bowl resting in the palm of the left hand symbolized the fact that one carries his good deeds into the after state with him, and that it is on the basis of his good deeds that his future status is to be determined. From this it is to be seen that they did not believe there was any forgiveness of sins, but rather that one must earn salvation for himself.

The settlement of Akkad having become a town, is was called Hur, from the Moon Goddess, which was the principal Divinity worshiped by the inhabitants. King Uruk raised a temple to her honor, which is an almost exact fac-simile of the temple erected to the God of the Sea, and also as a royal archive, at Chichen.

Hur grew to be a great center of Religion as well as of Commerce and Science, and it was here that the real Akkadian Civilization centered. In the later Centers of Life they were merging more toward the Chaldean or Babylonian Civilization, which was in reality nothing more than another and later development of that of the Akkadians.

The second capital of the Akkadians was situated twenty-five miles from Hur in a northwestern direction, on the east side of the Euphrates and about eight miles from its banks. This was built by King Urukh. The name of this city was Lallak, "lal" (companion) and "lak" (rude)—"the rude companion." In time the spelling of this name was changed from the Maya to the vernacular form and the result was the name became Larrak.

Some fifteen miles from Larrak, to the northwest and on the same side of the Euphrates, was built the Sacred City, where dwelt the God Anu and his wife Ishtar, and her Priestesses, the sacred courtesans. This city, sacred to Anu and Ishtar, was at first called Uruk from the name of its builder. Later it was changed into Erech and later into Warka.

Sixty-five miles from Uruk, on the east side of the Euphrates, thirty miles from its bank, on the edge of the Affej marshes, midway between that river and the Tigris, was erected the last great city of the Akkadians. This was Nibpul, "nib" (offering) and "ppul" (jar); that is, "the place where offerings of jars are made." The God Bel was the principal Divinity of this place and offerings of jars were made to him. This city flourished more than seven thousand years before Christ. Since that time it has been destroyed and four super-imposed cities have been built above its ruins, each one being built over the ruins of the one below it.

There was in Nippur a most extensive library, for some twenty-three thousand baked-clay tablets have been recovered from it. This library was situated in the Temple of Bel. There were also a great number of very valuable works of art, only a few of which have been recovered so far.

The city had the most improved methods of sanitation, equal to the best in Europe or America at the present time. They made use of the keystone arch and many other modern improvements.

Blue was the mourning color of these people. This is proven by the fact that many of the coffins still have a coating of blue glaze upon them. As blue was the mourning color of the Mayas, this is of great value as a proof that they were the same people as the Mayas.

Nippur was the seat of Akkadian Culture until the Akkadians were gradually transformed into the Chaldeans and erected the city of Babylon. Being Mayas in their descent, they preserved to a great extent the Maya system of government and society, though in the course of time the Feminism of the Mayas disappeared from among them, to give place to a more masculine form of society. Nevertheless, it was from these Akkadians that the primative Feminine impulse was derived which exercised so much influence over the ancient Orient. They were a Poetical and hence a Symbolic people, and therefore their form of government was based upon the Mystical Symbolism they had brought with them from Mayach. At the same time we are to bear in mind that their Civilization, partaking largely of the

Utilitarian form, was destined to cause them to lose sight of the more Spiritual element they had held in Mayach. One point, however, which is well for us to bear in mind is this—their form of government was a Theocracy. The real rulers of the country were the Gods. There was a Celestial Hierarchy that ruled in the Heavens, and this Celestial Hierarchy had its counterpart in the Terrestrial Hierarchy that ruled as their correspondent upon earth. From time to time their Theology underwent changes, so that first one, then another, God or Goddess had ascendance over the others, and the color of the Celestial Hierarchy was changed accordingly. This being the case, the Terrestrial Hierarchy was of necessity bound to change accordingly. This was the real reason why the government was never stable in its constitution. The King ruled as the Vizier of the Supreme God, and was His servant to do His Will. This being the case, there was never a permanent constitution to the country, for the Supreme Law of the Land, was the Will of the Divine Hierarch, who ruled the Gods as expressed through the King as His Hand and the High Priest as His Mouth Piece. As the God who ruled the Heavenly Hierarchy was not at all times the same, it followed that the complexion of the government changed that of the Celestial Hierarchy recognized by the Ruling Class. In many countries there is a definite principle which is universally accepted as the foundation of government, and any government that falls short of this principle has forfeited its right to exist. However, among the Akkadians this was not the case. The supreme law was the Will of the Gods. At the same time there was no definite authority among the Gods, first one and then the other was in the ascendancy. Now it was the duty of the King to express the Will of one of the gods above that of all the others it was at the head of the Hierarchy at that particular time. When the King established the Cultus of one of the gods above that of all the others it was assumed that that god had gained ascendancy over the others, and that the King was acting under his direction when he placed that Cultus above all the others. At the same time every one of the gods had His own particular nature; that is to say, an individuality of His own, and therefore the government must take particular tone when He ruled in the heavens. It was this principle which led to so many apparent contradictions in the form of government. It was the duty of the King to see that all served the gods and particularly the Chief God. Each city had its own Patron God, and for that reason when a city became the capital of the country its God was recognized as being the head of the Hierarchy, for if this were not the case how could it be that His city was at the head of all the cities in the nation? This becomes clear when we realize that Akkad was a Sacred Land, ruled absolutely by the gods, and, further, that its government and its geography were patterned absolutely after the heavens. The entire idea underlying the Akkadian system was to form on earth an exact counterpart of the Heavenly Hierarchy, and all of its Laws and Customs were derived from this idea and founded upon this laudable ambition. Of course the practical working out of this system was the placing of absolute and unquestioned power in the hands of the King.

Much of the Archaeological information contained in this article is to be found in The Word, issue of May, 1913, article "Origin of the Egyptians," by Dr. Le Plongeon, and all our readers are urged to procure the magazine and read that article. The author has made some use of said articles in procuring data for this contribution to the Maya History. However, the other matters, dealing as they do with the Inner Life of the Akkadians, are drawn from the Secret Archives of the Hermetic Brotherhood and are authentic in every detail.

CPSIA information can be obtained
at www.ICGtesting.com
Printed in the USA
LVIC062001100920
665451LV00006B/37